Ladybird

I'm Ready... to Look and Say!

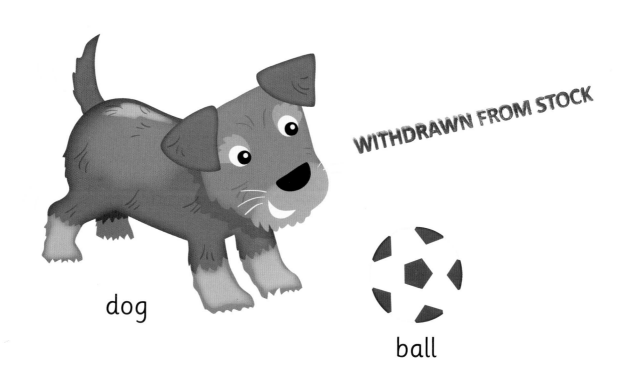

dog

ball

Illustrated by Ian Cunliffe

Educational consultant: Kate Ruttle

LADYBIRD BOOKS

UK | USA | Canada | Ireland | Australia
India | New Zealand | South Africa

Ladybird Books is part of the Penguin Random House group of companies
whose addresses can be found at global.penguinrandomhouse.com.

ladybird.com

Penguin
Random House
UK

First published 2015
001

Printed in China

A CIP catalogue record for this book is available from the British Library

ISBN: 978-0-723-29553-2

Contents

Notes for parents and carers

This is the ideal first words and pictures book for children starting nursery or school. The simple pictures and clear captions help your child to learn essential vocabulary and start linking words to images, an important pre-reading skill. The words are grouped by theme because that makes it easier for young children to remember and understand them.

This book also encourages children to think about the sounds that different objects make and to practise being good listeners. Learning to remember, imitate and tell the difference between noises they can hear around them ('environmental sounds') is a vital early stage of synthetic phonics and is taught in schools before the individual letter sounds are introduced.

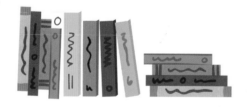

For more advice about phonics and for further activities visit: **www.ladybird.com**

Tips on how to use this book with your child:

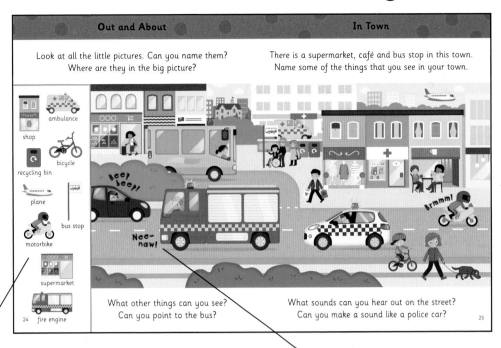

Read the simple question to your child and name the small pictures on the left-hand side. Can he find them in the main picture?

Using the instructions and questions, encourage your child to have fun naming the sounds she might be able to hear in the scene. The fire engine goes **NEE-NAW**!

Have fun pointing to the other objects in the big picture. Can your child name them all?

Use the scene in the picture to talk together.

What would you like to dress up as?

I'd love to be a dinosaur!

At Home

Look at all the little pictures. Can you name them?
Where are they in the big picture?

sofa

television

lamp

cat

cushion

flowers

newspaper

photograph

clock

slippers

Tick tock!

Miaow!

What other things can you see?
Can you point to the table?

The Living Room

Max and Olivia are playing a board game.
What do you like to do in your living room?

What sounds are there in the living room?
Can you make a sound like a cat?

At Home

Look at all the little pictures. Can you name them?
Where are they in the big picture?

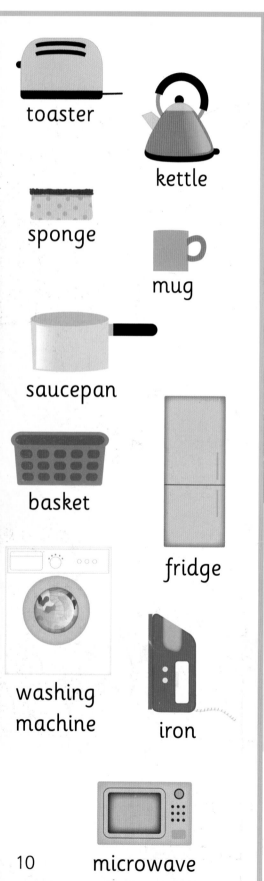

toaster

kettle

sponge

mug

saucepan

basket

fridge

washing machine

iron

microwave

What other things can you see?
Can you point to the sink?

The Kitchen

Dad is making a meal while Leo is doing his homework. What happens in your kitchen at home?

What sounds can you hear in a busy kitchen? Can you make a sound like a boiling kettle?

Look at all the little pictures. Can you name them?
Where are they in the big picture?

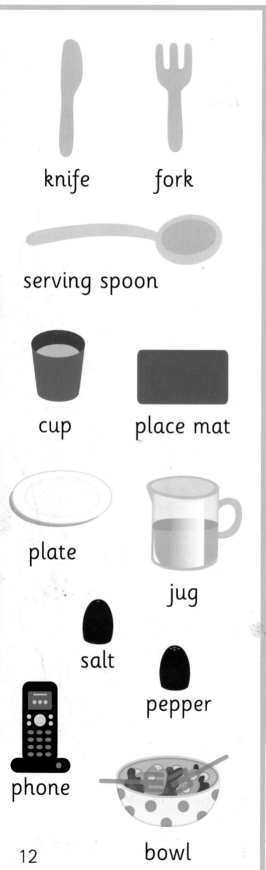

knife

fork

serving spoon

cup

place mat

plate

jug

salt

pepper

phone

bowl

12

Ring ring!

Mmmm!

What other things can you see?
Can you point to the peas?

The Dining Room

The family is eating a meal together.
What is your favourite thing to eat?

What noises can you hear in the dining room?
Can you make the sound of a knife and fork on a plate?

At Home

Look at all the little pictures. Can you name them?
Where are they in the big picture?

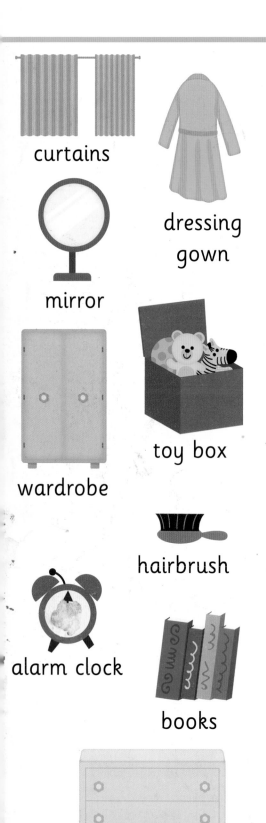

curtains

mirror

dressing gown

wardrobe

toy box

hairbrush

alarm clock

books

drawers

What other things can you see?
Can you point to the doll?

The Bedroom

Emily's alarm clock wakes her up every day.
Who helps you get up in the morning?

What sounds can you hear in your bedroom?
Can you make a yawn sound?

Look at all the little pictures. Can you name them?
Where are they in the big picture?

radiator

towel

toothbrush

shower

bath mat

laundry basket

toilet

potty

rubber duck

toilet brush

Glug!

What other things can you see?
Can you point to the bath?

The Bathroom

Jamie is brushing his teeth.
What else do you do in the bathroom?

What sounds are there in the bathroom?
Can you make a sound like a toilet flushing?

At Home

Can you match the objects on the right to the room they are found in?

Living Room

Kitchen

Dining Room

Bedroom

Bathroom

toaster	knife	fork	toy box
television	toilet	rubber duck	cat
wardrobe	lamp	hairbrush	potty
sofa	iron	laundry basket	shower
alarm clock	cushion	mirror	kettle
washing machine	radiator	jug	bowl

Look at all the little pictures. Can you name them?
Where are they in the big picture?

shed

bumblebee

butterfly

tree

ball

wheelbarrow

watering can

rake

lawnmower

bird

20

What other things can you see?
Can you point to the vegetables?

The Garden

Adam is playing football in the garden.
What do you like to do in your garden?

What different noises are there in the garden?
Can you make a sound like a ball being kicked?

Look at all the little pictures. Can you name them?
Where are they in the big picture?

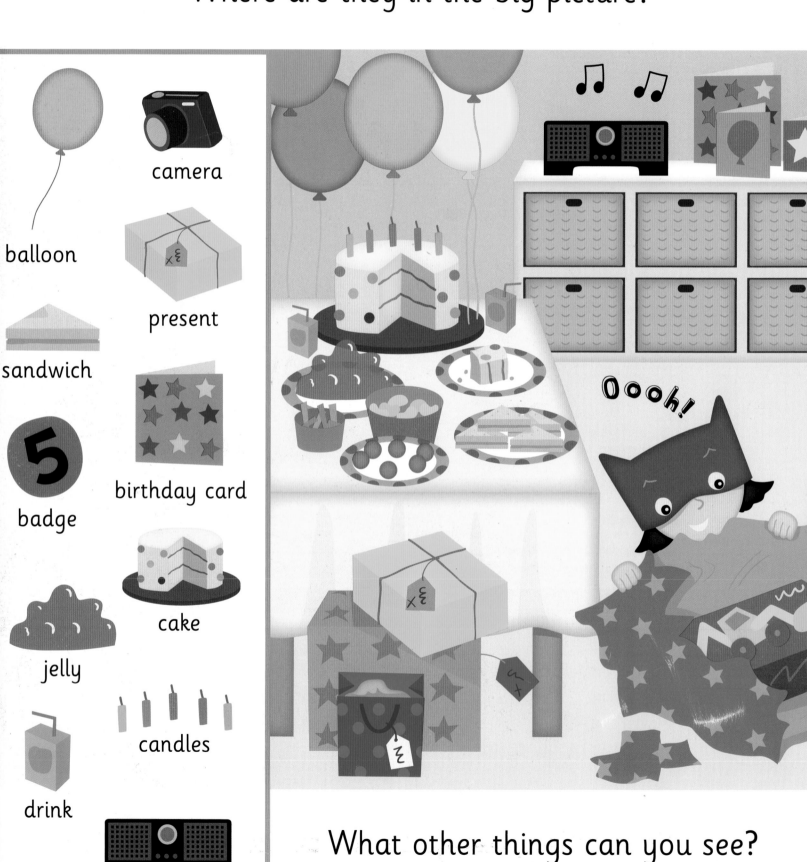

balloon

camera

present

sandwich

badge

5

birthday card

jelly

cake

candles

drink

music dock

Oooh!

22

What other things can you see?
Can you point to the wrapping paper?

A Party

All the children at the party are in fancy dress.
What would you like to dress up as?

What noises can you hear at the party?
Can you sing a song to wish someone happy birthday?

Look at all the little pictures. Can you name them?
Where are they in the big picture?

shop

ambulance

recycling bin

bicycle

plane

bus stop

motorbike

supermarket

Beep beep!

Nee-naw!

24 fire engine

What other things can you see?
Can you point to the bus?

In Town

There is a supermarket, café and bus stop in this town.
Name some of the things that you see in your town.

What sounds can you hear out on the street?
Can you make a sound like a police car?

Look at all the little pictures. Can you name them?
Where are they in the big picture?

trolley

fruit

till

card reader

bread

juice

fish

meat

shampoo

vegetables

basket

What other things can you see?
Can you point to the bananas?

The Supermarket

Daniel and his dad have bought eggs, milk and bread.
What does your family buy at the supermarket?

What sounds can you hear at the supermarket?
Can you make a sound like a trolley being pushed?

Look at all the little pictures. Can you name them?
Where are they in the big picture?

digger

spanner

drill

crane

toolbox

hard hat

brick

bucket

cement mixer

spade

bulldozer

Squeak!

What other things can you see?
Can you point to the wheelbarrow?

28

A Building Site

One of the builders is building a wall.
What are the other builders doing?

What things make a noise on a building site?
Can you make a sound like a digger?

Out and About

Can you match the objects on the right
to the places they are found?

Garden

Party

Town

Supermarket

Building Site

camera

ambulance

till

fire engine

lawnmower

watering can

hard hat

trolley

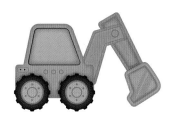
digger

present

bus stop

cement mixer

cake

tree

brick

ball

wheelbarrow

spanner

badge

sandwich

toolbox

jelly

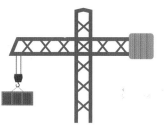
crane

music dock

Places I Go

Look at all the little pictures. Can you name them?
Where are they in the big picture?

stethoscope

scales

plant

magazine

computer

wheelchair

notice board

walking stick

printer

Da-dum da-dum!

Wrrr!

What other things can you see?
Can you point to the people waiting?

The Doctor's Surgery

The doctor is listening to the patient's heartbeat.
When have you had to see the doctor?

What noises can you hear at the doctor's surgery?
Can you make a sneezing sound?

Places I Go

Look at all the little pictures. Can you name them?
Where are they in the big picture?

train

coffee machine

suitcase

ticket

luggage

ticket machine

loudspeaker

taxi

departure board

ticket barrier

Bleep!

What other things can you see?
Can you point to the train drivers?

The Train Station

The red train is leaving the platform.
Where have you travelled to by train?

What sounds can you hear at the train station?
Can you make the sound of a train stopping?

Places I Go

Look at all the little pictures. Can you name them?
Where are they in the big picture?

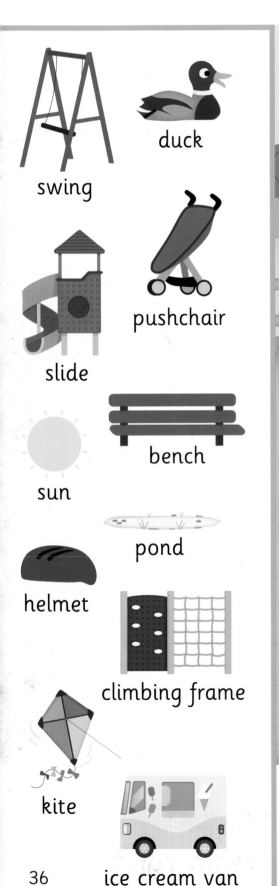

swing

duck

slide

pushchair

sun

bench

helmet

pond

climbing frame

kite

ice cream van

What other things can you see?
Can you point to the trees?

The Park

Can you see Claire coming down the slide? Point to her.
What is your favourite thing to do at the park?

What noises can you hear at the park?
Can you make a sound like an ice cream van?

Places I Go

Look at all the little pictures. Can you name them?
Where are they in the big pictures?

monkey

leaves

elephant

tyre
swing

giraffe

van

zoo
keeper

meat

log

lion

What other things can you see?
Can you point to the bucket?

The Zoo

The zoo keeper has come to check on the elephants.
What is your favourite animal?

What noises do the animals at the zoo make?
Can you make a sound like an elephant?

Places I Go

Look at all the little pictures. Can you name them?
Where are they in the big picture?

tractor

sheep

hen

pig

cow

farmer

goose

sheep dog

farm house

gate

Mooo!

Neigh!

Oin

What other things can you see?
Can you point to the fields?

The Farm

The horse is in the stable.
Where are the other animals?

What sounds can you hear on a farm?
Can you make a sound like a tractor?

Places I Go

Look at all the little pictures. Can you name them?
Where are they in the big picture?

sailing boat

spade

wind break

seaweed

sandcastle

beach ball

bucket

sun hat

umbrella

crab

rock pool

Snip snap!

What other things can you see?
Can you point to the sun?

The Seaside

Lily is building a sandcastle.
What do you like to do at the seaside?

What is noisy at the seaside?
Can you make a sound like the waves in the sea?

Places I Go

Look at all the little pictures. Can you name them? Where are they in the big picture?

whiteboard

drum

book

scissors

computer

paintbrush

blocks

chair

painting

computer mouse

reward stickers

tablet

Ummm

Splosh!

What other things can you see? Can you point to the teacher?

School

The children are busy playing and learning.
What is your favourite thing to do at school?

What sounds can you hear at school?
Can you make a sound like a drum?

Places I Go

Can you match the objects on the right to the places they are found?

Doctor's Surgery

Train Station

Park

Zoo

Farm

Seaside

School

46

ticket machine

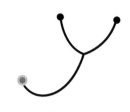
stethoscope

blocks

tractor

lion

ticket barrier

walking stick

swing

kite

cow

slide

sandcastle

ice cream van

meat

elephant

printer

duck

monkey

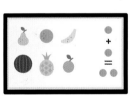
whiteboard

beach ball

umbrella

loudspeaker

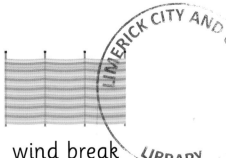
wind break

scissors

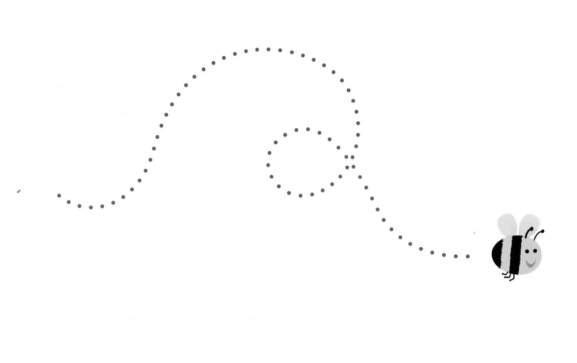